The Senses

written by Anne Giulieri

We use our senses to find out about things around us.
We use our eyes, ears, and mouth.
We also use our nose and hands.

Our five senses help us to find out about our world.

If we use our eyes, or *sense of sight*, we can look at things around us.

We can say:
It looks big.
It looks round.
It looks yellow.

Did You Know?
When a person can't see, they are called *blind* or *vision impaired*. Guide dogs help blind people.

If we use our ears, or *sense of hearing*, we can listen to the sounds around us.

We can say:
It sounds LOUD!
It sounds soft.

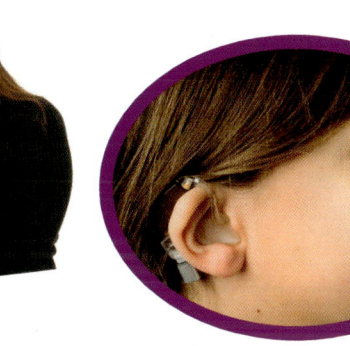

Some people are *deaf* or *hearing impaired*. These people can't hear sounds as others do. People who are deaf wear *hearing aids* or sometimes they use *sign language* to help them.

This is "I love you" in sign language.

If we use our mouth, or *sense of taste*, we can taste the food and drink around us.

We can say:

It tastes sweet.   It tastes salty.

It tastes bitter.

It tastes sour.

Did You Know?
We taste food and drink through our taste buds. Taste buds are the tiny bumps that cover our tongue.

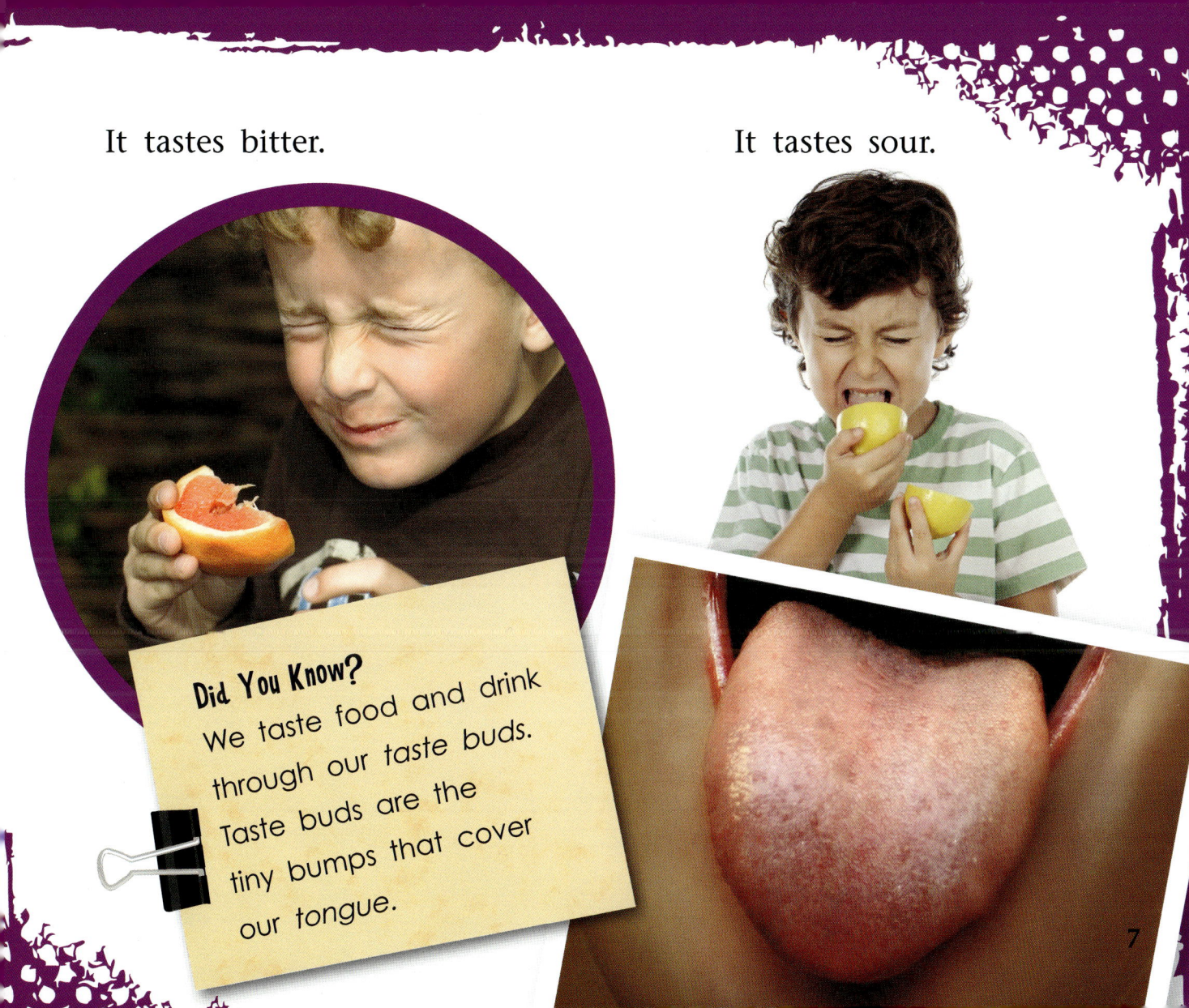

If we use our nose, or *sense of smell*, we can smell things around us.

We can say:
It smells like a flower.
It smells smoky.
It smells yucky!

Did You Know?
Girls can smell better than boys.

If we use our hands, or *sense of touch*, we can feel things around us.

We can say:
It feels soft.
It feels rough.
It feels hot.
It feels cold.

soft

Did You Know?
A baby's first sense is touch. A baby feels through his or her skin, hands, mouth, and tongue.

cold

rough

hot

Animals and Their Senses

Some animals have senses that are better than ours, while others have senses that are not as good.

Sight

We see colors such as red, orange, and yellow. We also see green, blue, indigo, and violet.

Did You Know? An owl can see 50 to 100 times better than us in dim light.

red
orange
yellow
green
blue
indigo
violet

What we see. What cats see.

Cats can only see black, white, or gray. But cats can see in the dark very easily when there is little light.

What we see. What cats see.

Hearing

We have ears on the side of our head for hearing.

Crickets have ears on their *knees*!

Bats, dogs, and dolphins have great hearing.

Did You Know?
Bats, dogs, and dolphins can hear sounds we can't hear.

Taste

We taste things by using our mouth and tongue. Flies and butterflies taste things through the little hairs on their feet! So when they land on something, they can taste it!

Worms do not have taste buds on a tongue. Instead, they have taste buds all over their body!

Smell

Did you know that bears, sharks, and dogs all have a much better sense of smell than we do? So do moths, snakes, and rats. Police dogs are trained to use their wonderful sense of smell to find things.

Touch

Cats use their *whiskers* to find out if a space is large enough for them to fit into. If their whiskers can fit, then they will fit, too!

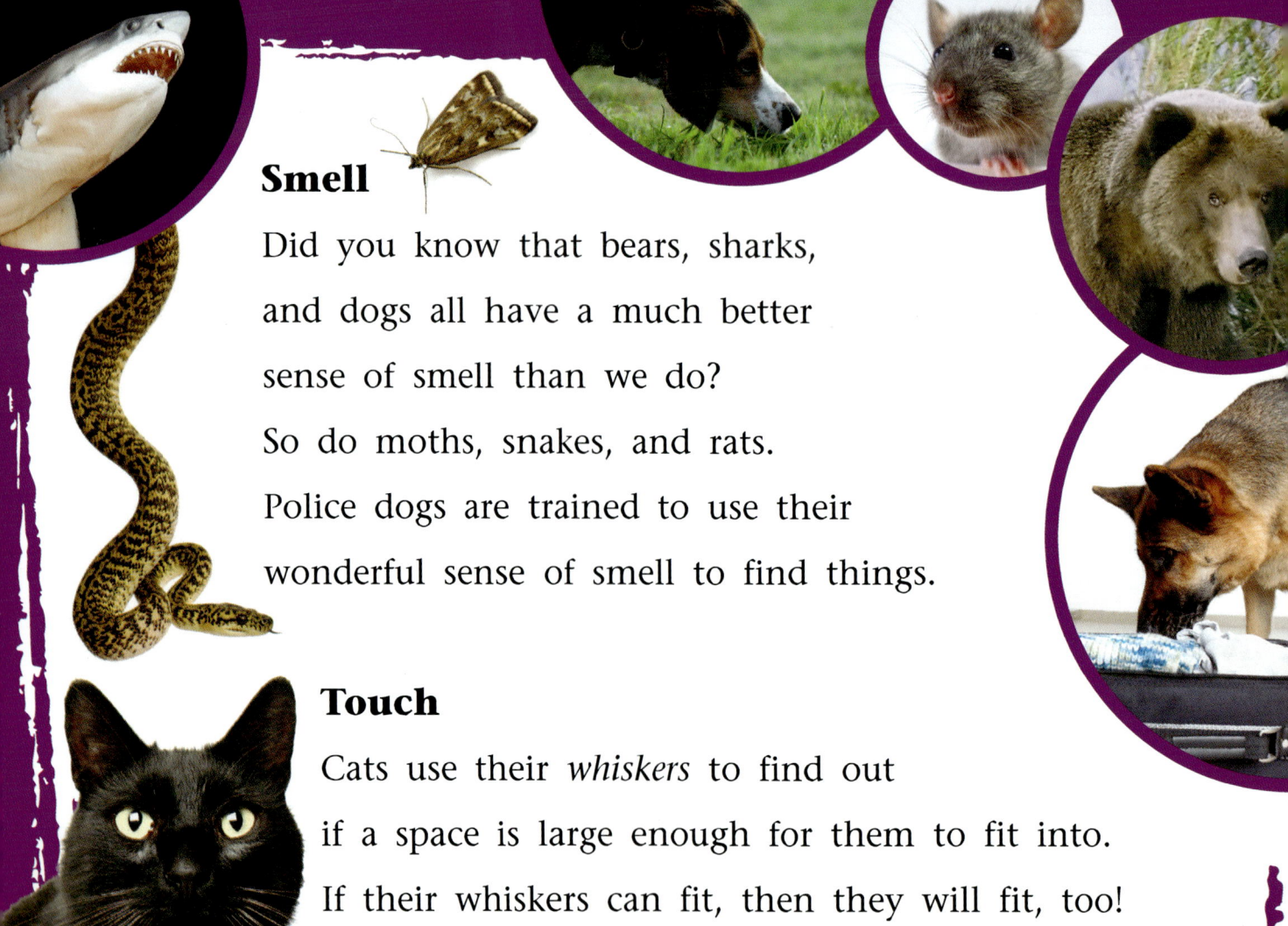

Because our senses help us in different ways, it is hard to know which sense is the most important. Which sense do you think is the most important?

Picture Glossary

 blind/vision impaired

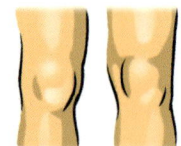 knees

 sense of taste

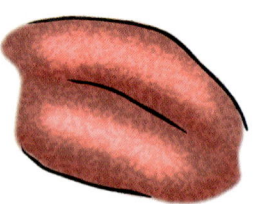 taste buds

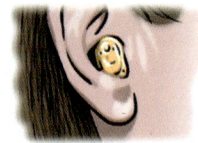 deaf/hearing impaired

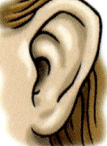 sense of hearing

 sense of touch

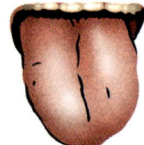 tongue

 guide dogs

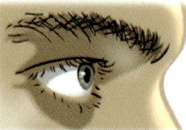 sense of sight

 sign language

 whiskers

 hearing aids

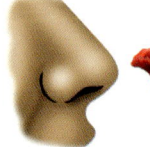 sense of smell

 skin

capstone
classroom

Engage Literacy is published by Capstone Classroom,
1710 Roe Crest Drive, North Mankato, Minnesota 56003.
www.capstoneclassroom.com

U.S. edition copyright © 2013 by Capstone Classroom, a division of Capstone.
All rights reserved.
No part of this publication may be reproduced in whole or in part, or stored in a retrieval system, or transmitted in any form or by any means, electronic, mechanical, photocopying, recording, or otherwise, without written permission of the publisher. For information regarding permission, write to Capstone Classroom, 1710 Roe Crest Drive, North Mankato, Minnesota 56003.

Originally published in Australia by Hinkler Education,
a division of Hinkler Books Pty Ltd,
Victoria, Australia, 3202.
www.hinklereducation.com.au

Text copyright © Anne Giulieri 2012
Illustration copyright © Hinkler Books Pty Ltd 2012

The Senses
ISBN: 978-1-62065-411-8

Acknowledgments
p2 (left): © Gabe Palmer | Dreamstime.com; p2 (right): © Petar Neychev | Dreamstime.com; p3 (far left): © Dreamzmaniac | Dreamstime.com; p3 (second from left) and p15 (second from right): © Howard Sandler | Dreamstime.com; p3 (top middle) and p15 (far right): © Ene | Dreamstime.com; p3 (second from right): © Rmarmion | Dreamstime.com; p3 (far right): © Elena Elisseeva | Dreamstime.com; p3 (bottom middle): iStockphoto.com / © Jaroslaw Wojcik; p4 (top right) and back cover: © Olegmit | Dreamstime.com; p4 (left, middle row): © Luchschen | Dreamstime.com; p4 (center of middle row): © Brad Calkins | Dreamstime.com; p4 (right, middle row): © Cynoclub | Dreamstime.com; p4 (bottom right): © Flirt / SuperStock; p5 (top right): iStockphoto.com / © Denis Zbukarev; p5 (left, middle row) and p15 (top middle): © Jose Manuel Gelpi Diaz | Dreamstime.com; p5 (center of middle row): © Richard Nelson | Dreamstime.com; p5 (right, middle row): © Phartisan | Dreamstime.com; p5 (bottom right): © Nancy Catherine Walker | Dreamstime.com; p6 (top right): © Dawn Balaban | Dreamstime.com; p6 (bottom left): © Yuri Arcurs | Dreamstime.com; p6 (bottom right): iStockphoto.com / © Doug Schneider; p7 (top right): © Martine De Graaf | Dreamstime.com; p7 (top right) and cover (center): © Jose Manuel Gelpi Diaz | Dreamstime.com; p7 (bottom right): © Maxwell De Araújo Rodrigues | Dreamstime.com; p8 (top right): © Rafal Olechowski | Dreamstime.com; p8 (middle), p15 (second from left) and cover (left): © Sandra Van Der Steen | Dreamstime.com; p8 (bottom left): © Glenda Powers | Dreamstime.com; p8 (bottom right): © Grecu Mihail Alin | Dreamstime.com; p9 (top right) and cover (right): © Esviesa | Dreamstime.com; p9 (top left) and p15 (top right): © Gamutstockimagespvtltd | Dreamstime.com; p9 (bottom right): © Lukatdb | Dreamstime.com; p9 (bottom, second from left): © Photowitch | Dreamstime.com; p9 (bottom, second from right): © Hans Slegers | Dreamstime.com; p9 (bottom right): iStockphoto / © Damir Cudic; p10: © Mircea Bezergheanu | Dreamstime.com; p12 (top right): iStockphoto / © Frank Rotthaus; p12 (top right): © Minden Pictures / SuperStock; p12 (bottom left): © Smellme | Dreamstime.com; p12 (bottom middle): © Potarou | Dreamstime.com; p12 (bottom right): © Istvan Budai | Dreamstime.com; p13 (top): © Sunfrog | Dreamstime.com; p13 (middle): © Andrey Klepikov | Dreamstime.com; p13 (bottom): iStockphoto / © John Shepherd; p14 (bottom left): iStockphoto / © Antagain; p14 (left, middle): iStockphoto / © Eric Isselée; p14 (top left): © Paul Banton | Dreamstime.com; p14 (top, second from left): © Anton Starikov | Dreamstime.com; p14 (top, middle): © Manicboy248 | Dreamstime.com; p14 (top, second from right): © Tamara Bauer | Dreamstime.com; p14 (top right): © Anthony Hathaway | Dreamstime.com; p14 (right, second from top): © Monika Wisniewska | Dreamstime.com; p15 (bottom middle): iStockphoto / © Donna Coleman

Printed in the United States 4379

Fluent
Level 20
Non-fiction

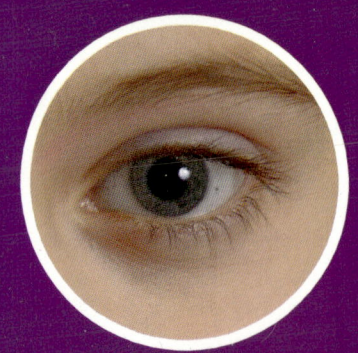

We use our eyes, ears, mouth, nose, and hands to find out about our world.
Which sense do you think is the most important?

Word count: 522
GRL: K